Government Choke Hold
But Who Are They Choking?

Butch Huff

authorHOUSE®

AuthorHouse™
1663 Liberty Drive, Suite 200
Bloomington, IN 47403
www.authorhouse.com
Phone: 1-800-839-8640

First published by AuthorHouse   9/4/2008

ISBN: 978-1-4389-0825-0 (sc)

Printed in the United States of America
Bloomington, Indiana

This book is printed on acid-free paper.

Government Choke Hold
But Who Are They Choking?

The government is choking themselves out of business or into another civil war. They are leaving the American people with nowhere else to turn but to fight our government. Release your choke hold and let us speak. I am not advocating a war; I am asking you to speak with your minds and your writing hand, not your guns, and not with violence.

The pen is truly mightier than the sword. There is only one person to vote for in this election and his name is Kirk Huff {please call me Butch} and as of now it will have to be a write in ballot; so instead of bitching about our government, it is time to do something about it. Read this book and then make your decision. I'm sure you will agree that the only way to get out of the mess we're in is to get someone into the White House who hates corrupt politicians and over taxation.

This might mean that you will have to get off of your butt and actually register to vote for the first time in years, or ever, but it will be worth it. Don't bitch if you don't vote. It's your right, use it. Enuff Is Enuff, vote for Huff. I am not a politician so I am asking you to read this book with an open mind. I don't have an ulterior reason for writing this, so I will be honest, even if it isn't popular. We have lost our freedom and it's time to get it back.

We need to change the way business is done or not done in Washington. That's what America really needs. We don't need some rich man or woman to tell us, the working class, how to spend our money. The only reason they get into politics is to benefit them. Why else do you think they spend millions of dollars to seek a job that only pays $400,000? Ask Bush with all his stock in oil and figure that one out. Do you think he made his money back? Yes, and then some!

I'm going to rant and rave all through this book so please forgive me for sounding rude or crude at times but this is how I truly feel. I am not a politician; in fact I hated politics growing up. It wasn't until about fifteen to twenty years ago that I started listening to what they were saying, and that's all it took. Blah, blah, blah, boring lies; not all lies but for the most part it was just a bunch of crap. Then I realized it wasn't entirely their fault. The President that we elect would submit a bill to congress and they would shoot it down. Well isn't that a bunch of bull. We vote them in because we believe they are going to do what say they're going to do, and Congress doesn't care. It's a big game in Washington D.C, and they need to start playing somewhere else.

Listen, you may not agree with my sarcastic and crude way of explaining things but I can guarantee you this, I won't bullshit you. Nothing but the truth, take it or leave it. It's yours to do with as you wish. But the fact is, I do care or I wouldn't be writing this book. I care about my family and friends and all the hard working people of the United States who are obviously **fed-up.** So if you care about your future, please read on with an open mind, and I am sure you will see that I'm nothing like any politician you've seen before because I'm not a politician.

We need to stop voting smooth talking lawyers into Congress and start electing business oriented people instead. No more long winded speeches filled with words lost in the dictionary that most people have never heard of. Get them the hell out of government; these lawyers are ruining this country. All they want to do is sue everyone and anyone. They write laws to benefit themselves and their colleagues. I have friends that are lawyers and I love them, but I don't love what they do. Defending hundreds of criminals they know are guilty before the one innocent one comes along, all at the taxpayer's expense. I don't blame them for their choice of occupation. Who wouldn't want to sit in a climate controlled environment and make the kind of money they do; it's the American way.

When the forty-nine states of America speak in November, maybe we'll get it right this time. Whoops! Did I say forty-nine states of America? Let me explain. Apparently we have forty-eight full states and two half states with Florida and Michigan. I guess their votes don't mean as much as the rest of the country. Well they do to me. I'm sorry that they have to put up with this nonsense. Let's hope this never happens in America ever again.

Why do we let this corruption go on in our country? This is our country not theirs, and yet we let politicians do this to us over and over again. This country needs to make the election process fair and easy. Why does Iowa and New Hampshire get to pick our president? Shouldn't we all have a say? Leave it to political parties to ruin everything. In the words of Jack Nicholson in Batman "This town needs an enema".

It's time to clean house and the Senate for that matter. No more 110 page bills filled with crap litigation and things that have absolutely nothing to do with the real purpose of the bill to begin with. I say we write a bill that says no more than two pages per bill which states the purpose of the bill and the reasoning behind it. Keep it straight and to the point with no strings attached. One bill for one thing. No hiding something in a 110 page document like they do now. Now that would be a real change.

I hate political parties; it's the lazy man's way to vote. You've got your own mind use it. I hate the fact that we have to pick a party when we register to vote. I don't know how I'll vote until I hear what they have to say. After that I'll choose which candidate I like, not which party. Don't be lazy you're better than that.

If you're not pissed at me yet, give me a chance; I've got lots to say, and I'm sure somewhere in this book I'll get you a little upset, but that's freedom of speech and we need to use our freedom to get rid of business as usual in Washington.

Please read on and remember.

Table Of Contents

Overview

First of all I am not spending one dime of tax payer's money on this campaign. Second, I am only spending a few dollars for the web site; the rest I am doing myself. I don't have speech writers or someone writing this for me. This is 100% me and no one else, except for the help of spell check, and my own research of other peoples' work. So if you should disagree with me or think that I am an idiot, I would presume you to be a lawyer, politician or insurance salesmen.

Throughout this book I will explain why I feel there should be a federal ID card and why it will help. I will talk about taxes and the so called fair tax and why I think it's a joke.

I will also talk about my plans for jobs, health care, housing, insurance and lottery reform, as well as interest rates on credit cards. I will explain my views on such topics as: abortion, gay marriage, and gun control.

And finally I will talk about the future, technology and how we need to get rid of No Child Left Behind and do more with the education programs.

Retirement is something that far too many people are not prepared for. I will explain how every working person can retire wealthy.

There are no quick fixes for anything but now is a good time to start. I don't expect you to agree with everything, but I hope that most of you agree on what is really important - your money, your health, and your future.

There are far too many problems in this world to talk about all of them, but I will tell you some things that matter to me.

Right now, there is a lot of talk by all the candidates about how they feel about a gas holiday. Obama is against it because it will take away from the roads and bridges and is a short term gimmick. Clinton is for it but wants to charge oil companies in some way, and McCain simply wants to give a gas tax break. I love it. First of all, we built this country long before there ever was a gas tax, so if you ask me, both Mc-Cain and Clinton are right. However Obama says no. What else will he say no to?

The fact is our taxes have been going up since they started taxing us, and it really hasn't been all that long. More and more government is the reason our taxes are so high. I am not so much against big government as much as I'm against the misuse of government. Government misuse of funds is a huge problem. With hundred dollar hammers and toilet seats, it's no wonder they're going broke. But that's just a small part of it. The problem I see with government is they like to give handouts to other countries in need before taking care of their own.

Also the government likes to pay their employees very well. The fact is too well. First of all they're not government employees, they're our employees. We pay them with our tax dollars. Why do they get the best health care? Why do they get great vacation and sick leave benefits? Why can't their retirement fund be tapped into like our Social Security fund has? Why do they set our minimum wage way below the lowest pay grade that they have for themselves? Why? Why? Why?

The federal government is too big in all the wrong places. Too many chiefs and not enough Indians. Don't take that wrong. I've got a little Indian in me. And I've had a little of me in a couple of them. Bad joke.

We have to stop wasteful spending and treat every American equally. Taxpayers' dollars shouldn't be paying for someone else to have a better life than them.

There are many laws I disagree with, one of which is the law on sex. Sex is personal, stay out of it. If people want to have sex, they're going to and who cares? We wouldn't be here if it weren't for sex. When did we start regulating it anyway? And why did we start regulating it? I agree with the age part mostly with exception to an 18 year old and a 16 year old who could very well be in the same grade in school or have been dating since they were 14 and 16. After that, it's fair game between willing parties.

We all know what's right and wrong in a relationship but that's not the government's place to exploit someone else's affairs. That is between the parties involved, period. The reason I bring this up is because the D.C. madam just committed suicide, or was shut up by some government official and made to look like suicide. Either way, it's not the government's business whom people are having sex with. They're just pissed they didn't get any or that they couldn't tax it, or even watch for some. Why is it that we are so worried about who's sleeping with who anyway? Is it jealousy or just a way to waste tax payer's dollars in the courtroom?

Seat belts and motorcycle helmets, this pisses me off too. Why do they feel they have the right to protect me from getting hurt in a car or motorcycle accident, when someone can walk into Wal-Mart, buy a rifle and shells, walk outside and shoot somebody? This makes absolutely no sense to me. It's all because insurance companies are protecting their investments. Saving them money and hopefully our lives, true, but mostly to save them money.

They lobbied that the reason the cost of insurance was so high, was because it cost too much to take care of the injured motorist. They argued that by saving lives and cutting down the injuries by wearing these safety devices they could save money and in turn save us money. When has your insurance gone down? Exactly, it hasn't. Something has to be done.

Have you ever worn a motorcycle helmet on a hot sunny day? That's not exactly safe either. A helmet is made of Styrofoam, which is an insulator. This not only holds your body heat in, but when the sun is beating down on you, it makes you a lot hotter. Ever hear of heat stroke?

Why is it when you get a traffic ticket, the cost of the court charge is usually higher than the fine? And why is the cost of court so high when your turn in front of the judge only takes 30 seconds? How does 30 seconds or even 2 minutes translate into $125? It's down right ridiculous. Who is the criminal in this case? The government is. That's enough of that.

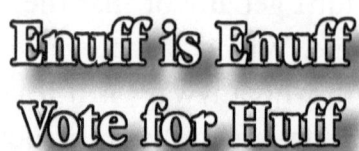

Some Thoughts Before Getting Started

I have always been somewhat of a dreamer. I have always tried to invent things and make things better. I don't actually think that I will be elected president and I never even really wanted to be the president anyway. Besides that, I would need a girdle and 10 pounds of make-up just to make me look halfway decent at a press conference. Also, I wouldn't want to wear a suit and tie everyday. Just give me a pair of jeans and a t-shirt and I'll be just fine. But, I am so sick of the things that go on in this country that I had to write this book and say what's on my mind.

We have heard about the carburetor that gets a hundred miles to the gallon, and the car that runs on water. We have also heard the stories of those people getting killed, or having so called accidents. Government cover ups happen all the time. What is the government afraid of? We used to be the innovators. We used to be the industrial capital of the world. What happened? Greed and government happened.

Some of my ideas in this segment go against what you will read later, but remember these are just some of my ideas on life and politics. So with that being said, let me express myself.

I love life. I love people, and I love having fun. Life should be fun; there is no use in being miserable, because life is way to short. The world is not getting bigger, but we as a people are multiplying way too fast. We are having children way too early in life and we are living longer. I never got to meet my great-grandparents, but kids today are meeting their great-great-grandparents. While this might seem great to some, it is sad to me. This means five generations of kids in less than hundred years. This bothers me because we are over populating the world. I'm pretty sure that these kids having kids are not getting the education they need, and they're not old enough or experienced in life to raise a child properly in today's society.

I am a firm believer that you should not have kids until you are at least twenty one and closer to twenty five. Get your education first and then get a job before taking on the responsibility of someone else's life before you have taken responsibility of your own.

With the rich getting richer and the poor getting poorer, it now takes two salaries or more just to make ends meet. With both parents working, who is left to raise the children? Who's taking care of the children when you're at work and what kind of guidance are they getting? It scares me. I see it all the time; parents are too exhausted to care, so they just use the television sitter. That's a good one. No wonder these kids are wearing their pants half way down their ass, or grabbing their crotches like Michael Jackson did in his videos and Madonna in her videos. Even now, she doesn't like them. Too late, already said and done. Thanks for screwing up our kids. What kind of parent lets that happen, not me? No, I'm not a saint, far from it, but certain things must stay true, such as manners and being accountable for your actions. The golden rule should always apply.

With regards to both parents having to work in today's society and the over population with busy streets and grid lock, just plan no time to do anything. One idea I have had, was having four shifts in a day instead of three. It makes sense to me, and I'll tell you why. Just think of the possibilities we could have with six hour work days. First, you could actually get a full night's rest. Eight hours of actual sleep which would help with a lot of the health problems we have today. Second, it would give you more time to get to and from work. Hopefully, this would help relieve traffic congestion, road rage, and the stress of driving. Again, less stress is good for your health. Then, there is the fatigue factor at work. Less time at work, less fatigue, and the end result is a better product, not to mention that there would be another shift added to every company which in turn would **create more jobs**. After all that, you would have more family time, and that is the most important thing of all. Of course, this idea diminishes my plan for retirement but it's just an idea of mine.

Next, I feel that government doesn't want free power, such as: totally electric cars or a car that runs on water or even the compressed air engine. Why don't they want free power? Because they can't tax free power. They just don't see the benefits of free power the same way as I do. Before we go any further, I would like you to put a book mark on this page and go to your computer and log onto www.lutec.com.au. They have got an electric motor that increases power by the use of magnets. Magnetic power is the future; it doesn't burn any fuel and it's free and clean. I'll see you in a few minutes.

Pretty cool isn't it? I love the Internet. Now the government can't hide things like they used to. Unlimited knowledge right at your finger tips. The information era will soon change the world we live in. After all, the government can't kill everyone, or can they?

If we could run our cars for free, oil companies would have a fit. There would still be a need for oil for the more important things that oil is used for, like soaps, plastics, and many other petroleum based products we use in every day life.

This means we could use our own oil instead of the Arabs'. Now that makes more sense to me. By not buying oil from the Arabs, we could solve two problems at once. The Arabs would take a huge blow to their economy, and we would be more self-sufficient. Also, the price of oil would drop to all time lows, which would lower the price of plastics, soaps and other petroleum based products.

Why should we support the Arabs that are helping the terrorist get supplies anyway? We shouldn't.

It could take at least ten years to replace all the cars and trucks in this country, so the need for oil will still be here for some time to come. Big oil companies shouldn't panic; there will always be a need for oil.

Free power would mean lower shipping costs, which in turn lowers the cost of goods, which puts more money in your pocket to spend on other things that help boost our economy. So, instead of sending all the gas money to countries we're fighting, we could be spending that money here in our own country and starve out the countries we're fighting.

If we had free power, we could travel anywhere we wanted to, and it would not cost anything but time. Of course, we would wear out the tires a lot faster putting tire manufacture's to work. That's a good thing. We would have to eat on the road and stay at hotels. That's another good thing. The service industry would boom. Auto makers would no longer have EPA restrictions or fuel mileage to worry about. That would mean they could actually not worry about the aero dynamic design that goes into the cars today. Therefore, the auto industry could have more creative body styles. We could possibly get back to when the body styles changed more frequently like back in the 50's. Hey, that would put more people back to work. Wow! With all these people working I don't think we would have a tax problem, do you?

While I'm on the subject of cars, did you hear about the car GM is working on that actually drives itself? Yes it's true. Does this mean if you're out having a good time and have one too many that you could actually sit in the passenger seat and get a free ride home? No more driving under the influence tickets. Poor lawyers will have to find something else to do. Come to think of it so will the cops. Maybe they could make our neighborhoods safer by patrolling them instead of the highways. Isn't that what they were supposed to do from the beginning?

Nothing I hate more than seeing a cop on the divided highway pulling someone over for 75 in a 65 when I can't get the cops to stop people from doing 55 in a 35 on my street, with my kids and the neighbor's kids out playing, this really pisses me off. Well enough about that. Now let me talk about the fair tax. Ha ha ha.

Fair tax and getting rid of the IRS go hand in hand. It can't be done. First of all, who is going to make sure that these taxes are enforced? Hmm, would that be the IRS or would we just give them a new title? Give me a break; as long as there is going to be a tax of any kind, there will be some sort of IRS. Don't be fooled by any scheme that you read about a fair tax; who is it fair to? The rich and well off. No, just the rich. How much money can you spend if you have millions in the bank? If you have millions in the bank, you make more in interest per year than most people make all year. Plus they got rich by not spending their money. Think of it this way, if you already have everything, then what are you going to buy? The answer is nothing; that's right, nothing.

What? Do you think they need two of everything? I don't think so. When they have that much money and everything that they need, the only thing left to do is travel, and they're not traveling the states. They are traveling the world spending their money elsewhere, so please don't tell me the fair tax is fair. The fair tax is a joke. Besides that, the 23% tax they talk about is actually 25% or more. How or why? You would now be paying tax on their tax. Don't get it yet? Let me explain: if you buy a hundred dollar coat with the 23% tax already included and you pay 7% sales tax in your state then that means your state made an extra 1.24%. Still confused? So am I. You're paying tax on tax. If the $100 coat already has the 23% federal tax included, and then you paid 7% on their 23% which is actually another 1.24% for your state, the state would love it. It's confusing I know. Well its time for me to act like Ross Perot with a bunch of charts that you will see throughout this book, but it makes it easier to understand for some.

The first line is a coat costing $81.30; the fair tax of 23% brings the cost to $100 which you purchase and pay an additional 7% state tax on for a total of $107.00.

	cost	fed tax	cost to you	state tax	total
Coat	$81.30	23.00%	$100.00	7.00%	$107.00
		fed & state	total		
Coat	$81.30	30.00%	$105.69	1.24%	$107.00
Coat	$81.30	31.61%	$107.00		

Now take that same coat that cost $81.30 and put the two taxes together for a total of 30% and you save 1.24 % Huh! Wait it gets worse now take that same coat $81.30 and the final price their way $107.00 and its 31.61% tax. Is it me or did we lose a third of a percent in mid air? Joke, Joke, Joke, It's a Joke. Who do they think they're fooling? Fair tax with Social Security figured into it. How the hell is that going to get split up? Some for me, and more for them. If you believe that, I've got a bridge for you, bought and paid for by the US government. It's called the bridge to nowhere and it can be yours, because you're the next contestant on the new tax yourself to death. That's right, just come on down; we'll start the bidding at 4 years and if he or she is as bad as the last one, then we'll just give them another 4 years to let them make up for it. Hell, it worked really well this time. I am a sarcastic son of a bitch, but I can't help it. My mother didn't raise no fool, she raised 5 of them. Love ya Momma.

Neal Boortz says that he wants to give tax rebates to everyone, every month, including the rich. Oh what group of government employees is going to do that? Let's see, he fired the IRS so he must have rehired them to write checks or as they claim, put money on your debit cards.

Let me put it to you this way; if rich people have everything they need, and get extra money from the government every month. If all they needed to buy was food. Where would the government get their tax money from? Oh you finally got it. That's right, us, the working class people. Not the rich and well off.

Don't you think that if this fair tax bill were to be approved, that all the rich people would buy everything new with extended warranties before the tax would go into effect anyway? If that happened, the government would be broke in a couple of years. Oh yeah! They're already broke. Give me a break, he's a talk show host working with a politician, say one thing and mean another.

Have you ever noticed that when one thing goes up on one end, it's an excuse to mark it up on the other? Ok, I buy a pound of raw material for .813 cents a pound. After the government gets their 23%, it now cost me $1 a pound. I then raise my price a little more because that's just the way it has always been. It cost me a little more so I'll tack on a little more, and sells it to someone else who adds a little more; forget it, its crazy. The cost of goods will be so high it's not funny. I just bought a shovel before the fair tax becomes reality and the first thing I'm going to do is bury that book. I probably could burn it cheaper or better yet be politically correct and recycled it. Don't get caught up in this crap, we're already brain washed as it is. Wake up. This brings me to my next gripe political parties.

Political parties, Why, Why, Why? Political parties, you've got to be kidding me, right? The true answer is that most of you are lazy. My father is a Republican, so that means that I am a Republican. My mother is a Democratic, so that means I'm a Democrat. Give me a break; I hate to say it but you were born with your own brain, and if you don't start using it we're all going to be in trouble.

I like a little bit of both sides and I hate a little bit from both sides, but I'm voting for the one who says they're going to do what I believe is right. Not for a party, because it stands for this or that. I have listened to all the debates from both sides, and I picked who I felt would be the best one, and as of now I'm not liking any of them.

I don't mean to put down the Republican Party but, ok, yes I do. I don't understand how they can be so dead set against abortion and at the same time be all for the right to bare arms, and they're the biggest supporters of the military who kill thousands of innocent people, including our own. Don't get me wrong; I don't like abortion either but then again nobody does.

Don't be lazy; vote for the best candidate, not a political party.

Also, try and run for office without belonging to a party and see what happens. It is not fair the way the government is set up and it needs to change. I say no parties. Let people run on their own beliefs, and let's hear what they have to say. Let's give equal time to each candidate, and narrow it down from there. I have been independent for years, but now they call it a party too. So now, I'm just left out.

I was listening to Glenn Beck on CNN cry over some economist saying that we'll never get out of this debt. The fact is we will get out with hard work, and good direction. They said we wouldn't come out from the last Bush, but we did. How? We raised minimum wage, which then increased spending, which made more jobs, which in turn raised the tax base. It can be done. With the price of gas out of sight, inflation has sky rocketed and killed the economy. We can't afford to drive to work. The price of oil has done the same thing that the fair tax would do, take all of our money.

Because fuel costs more, shipping costs more, and then the price just keeps going up. Everyone has to get their own piece of the pie. It happens all the time; that's business. A bar owner pays $12 a case for 24 bottles of beer it cost him .50 cents a bottle and he sells it for $1 now it goes up to $14 a case which is less than .10 cents a bottle but he goes up to a $1.25 that's the way it works. I can't say it enough, I hate the fair tax. How did I get back on the fair tax? Sorry I'm still burning from reading it. But that's the reason I'm writing this book, so I should thank him.

Why is it, the worse your credit is, the more they charge you? It makes no sense; they raise the rate based on your score. When you start at 12% with a score of 680, and then you spend on your card, which puts a strain on your debt to income ratio, your credit score drops a little, and your interest rate goes up. That is crazy; we need some kind of reform. The credit card companies are killing us. There should be a cap of no more than 15% on any type of loan company period.

Insurance is one of the topics I hate the most. I hate insurance companies. To me they are nothing but organized crime. All they do is take your money. However, when the time comes to make a claim, watch and see what happens. They try to find every reason in the world not to pay you the full amount. First, they spend more money trying to discredit your claim with some over paid investigator. Then, when you include your deductible, you lose. They victimize you twice; first you're the victim of an accident, fire, or theft and then you get victimized by your insurance company.

I also feel as though insurance is another form of tax. Why do I feel that it is a tax? That's because our government forces us to have it. If they force us to pay for something, it's a tax. Ok, I have had this argument with many people, and they say it is not a tax. I said "If you drive a car, do you have to have insurance?" They answered yes. Then they said don't drive. Well, I guess we should all go back to the horse and buggy. That would make a nice odor on your daily drive to work. Then the government would make you clean up after your horse, and auto companies would lay everybody off. Then, everyone who makes parts for the auto companies would get laid off, and we would all lose our houses to the local government for not being able too pay the taxes. I can't breathe, you're choking me to death, and this whole thing smells like horse shit.

Don't be afraid of technology. Just because technology may cut some jobs, it always creates new jobs too. Don't think that robots will some day rule the earth; they just might make it easier.

First of all we need jobs. Without jobs, we have no tax base. Without a tax base, we have a weak and defenseless country. We need a product, not just paper. We are becoming the paper work capital of the world. We need products; we need industry. We need something we can sell; not lawyers and litigation costing tax payers' money for the pockets of their colleagues. Example; Roger Clemens steroid case is a big waste of tax payer's money, and yes, I care about the integrity of the game, but not at the tax payers' expense. Let baseball pay for it; they have the money, not us.

Second, we need a federal I.D card insuring that you are a legal U.S citizen or tax paying worker here on a legal work visa. If you are here legally, you will need this I.D card to get a legal job, health care, and qualify you for a special interest rate for housing.

We need stiff fines, not jail for people hiring illegal workers. Putting them in jail just costs more of your tax dollars. Jails need to be for dangerous felons, not the working class tax paying Americans with families. There are a lot of people in jail that wouldn't harm a flea, but they're in jail unable to work, and support their families for not paying traffic fines, driving without insurance, taxes, and so on. All they are doing is trying to make an honest living for their family in this corrupt, over taxed country that we live in. How in the hell are they going to get tax money from someone in jail? They're not.

Third we need a tax system that works. Not a fair tax. We have over 350 tax credits, or breaks according to Turbo Tax; this is crazy. I will explain how my tax system would help everyone, including businesses and still be fair.

Finally, we need health care that works. All the candidates talk about it, but that is all they do, talk. Also, how do they plan on funding it? They will probably raise our taxes, and or force us to pay for it some other way. They try to sell us a great idea without any solutions (like No Child Left Behind – hang on).

Please take the time to read each and every issue that I discuss in this book with an open mind. Don't be too quick to judge, and please don't quit just because you may disagree with one topic or another. When you finish, I'm sure that most of you will agree that I would make the best choice for **President of the United States**. By the way, if I got the call at 3:00 a.m., I would say "I'm busy right now. Can I call you back in 20 minutes?"

Enuff is Enuff
Vote for Huff

Federal ID Card

The federal ID card is not my idea; however, I do support it. My idea for the card is a little more complex than what others might have in mind. Friends of mine say we already have a federal ID card; it's called the Social Security card. While this might be true to some degree, the card does not have your picture on it. Therefore, anyone can make a fake ID card to get a job with a card like that.

However, with the information age and the ID card that I would use, it would be like a credit card with your picture on it. When you set up this card, it will contain information as to where to send your retirement fund. Yes, retirement fund is the new way of saying Social Security and I'll explain more on that later in that section. The Federal ID will have your picture and number on it, along with your thumb print, and a magnetic strip on the back. This card will make it nearly impossible to get a job without it.

In this day and age, nearly every company or small business in the world has a computer. Therefore, in order to get a job in the United States, you will need to have one of these cards. If you're illegal, you can't get a card. Therefore, have fun trying to get a job; it's that simple.

Also, a lot of criminals on the loose will have a tough time getting work because once they scan the card, if they can even get a card, the state and federal government will know where to look for them. Therefore, they will have no place to go.

In addition to that, with my retirement plan, you will insist on working on the books instead of under the table because your future will depend on it. I will show you how beneficial it is for you to do so.

What's more, this card will insure that if you need medical attention, you will be taken care of. This card that I would propose would also make it harder for doctors and hospitals to cheat the health care system. Not that it can't be done, there are always ways to cheat. We just have to make it harder.

Every time that you go to the doctor or hospital, you will need to use this card. By using this card, it will assure the government that it is you being treated. That way, there isn't any possibility of fraud by another individual, a doctor or hospital.

So many people get talked into working under the table by small businesses. That's because businesses don't want to deal with all the added expenses that go into a pay check. They always say that $8 per hour cash is like $10 on the books. Let's put that to the test.

Under the current tax system in North Carolina, $8 per hour for ten hours would gross $80 and $10 would gross $100. Now if we take your Social Security out of the hundred dollars, you're left with $92.45. Then take out state and federal taxes on that amount, you would be left with around $85. So actually, you end up a little short. Then, deduct all the insurances that the employer would have to have on you, depending on your type of work. You can then see why it is easier for the employer to pay you cash. However, in the end, it's you that ends up a little short. So now, the only one who loses is you.

The employer saves all the insurance and tax money. Then add in the matching Social Security that they would have to pay on you, but ends up paying the Social Security on themselves. This makes it better for them, but ends up hurting you and your Social Security.

Plus, if you get hurt at work, you're screwed because technically you are not employed, and it will cost you plenty to try and get compensated. When you're young, you don't think about things like that. All you think about is the fact that you're making pretty good money, but when it comes down to it, you're not.

Also, when it comes time to get a loan and you need documentation of employment, you get hit upside the head by the bank when they want tax records you don't have. It is then that you realize that it's not worth it. That's the governments' fault for making it so hard on employers to do business with this crazy tax code that makes no sense at all. Add that to all the insurances they force you to have, and you can see why we are losing jobs to foreign countries.

Between sending money to State and Federal tax commissions, they also have to pay Social Security and workman's compensation insurance. No wonder small business are having trouble competing.

This card is your life. It is your job, your retirement money, and your health. This card could be the best way to stop illegal immigrants from getting your jobs and wasting our tax payer dollars.

If we could get everyone working legally, paying taxes and building their own retirement. This government would be a smooth running machine.

I'll explain throughout this book why you will want to have this card. I'm sure when you read further it will make more sense as to why we should have it.

**Enuff is Enuff
Vote for Huff**

Taxes

First of all, no one should ever have to go to jail over taxes, period. I would pardon all tax offenders immediately; they are not hardened criminals, and it costs more to house them in jail than they probably owe. Wesley Snipes isn't a trouble maker; let him out and give him a chance to repay. There has got to be a better way to run this government. The United States houses more prisoners than any other country in the world. And we call them communist; think about that.

I have a few ideas that would make it easier and less of a hassle to pay taxes. Doing your taxes should not be costly or a nuisance to anyone. As Americans we don't mind being taxed. We just don't want to be over taxed. I would get rid of some or most of the IRS and the tax system as we know it. No more tax refunds or right offs, just a straight tax. No more filing joint, single, married, or claiming kids; just a straight non refundable tax, based on your income. This would eliminate several government jobs, saving your tax dollars and helping to lower taxes.

I would have a 5% federal sales tax (except on groceries, clothing items under $50 per item, and automobiles under $40,000). I would also lower every tax bracket by 5% to 10%. I think that a federal sales tax would be a major contributor to the tax fund; however, I feel it should be kept low at 5%, and never, and I mean never, go up from there. There is no reason to raise this tax, because when the costs of goods go up, so do the profits from taxes.

Let me explain. If you buy a watch for $10, you would pay fifty cents federal tax. Now take the exact same watch five years later, costing $15 dollars because of inflation, or whatever. Then you would pay seventy-five cents federal tax. So, there is no reason to ever change that amount. When inflation goes up, so does the profit of tax.

The main reason I'd want to keep it so low is so that it would not hurt low income families. Another reason for keeping it so low is so that it wouldn't hurt the tourism industry, and discourage tourists from coming to the states.

The 5% federal sales tax will help collect money from all kinds of people, from hard working taxpayers, to people working jobs off the books, from illegal workers, as well as tourists. This would be a huge boost in government revenue without, over taxation. This 5% federal sales tax would allow for the cut in your federal payroll tax, along with the straight tax, which would help in eliminating some or most of the IRS.

The straight tax is like a flat tax, but scaled similarly to the tax scale we have now. It is not a so called fair tax or flat tax such as Steve Forbes tried to push years ago, and Neal Boortz is doing now. My straight tax plan is just that, pay it and you're done. No more claiming kids or interest on mortgages. No more claiming married or single with children. No more accountant fees at the end of the year. No worrying about being audited and having your life taken away. It is a non discriminative tax. Everyone pays. Keep the government out of your life.

Businesses will still be subject to claming things and write-offs, but they too will get taxed less under my plan, and will also save. Anyone who claims they can get rid of the IRS completely is lying through their teeth. As long as we have taxes, we will have some sort of IRS; don't be fooled.

Government should not tax utilities. Utilities are a necessity, and should not be taxed. I also feel that there shouldn't be any taxes higher than 25% on anyone or anything, including capital gains, inheritance taxes, or lottery winnings. No tax over 25%, period. If the government can't work with that, then they need to get out of government business. No refunds, exemptions, or breaks. No taxes on your retirement fund until you draw. I will discuss lottery taxes later in that section.

Below is a chart showing the government poverty level for 2007.

2007 HHS Poverty Guidelines

Persons in Family or Household	48 Contiguous States and D.C.	Alaska	Hawaii
1	$10,210	$12,770	$11,750
2	13,690	17,120	15,750
3	17,170	21,470	19,750
4	20,650	25,820	23,750
5	24,130	30,170	27,750
6	27,610	34,520	31,750
7	31,090	38,870	35,750
8	34,570	43,220	39,750
For each additional person, add	3,480	4,350	4,000

SOURCE: *Federal Register, Vol. 72, No. 15, January 24, 2007, pp. 3147–3148*

Below is a tax table that I think would be fair to everyone. First of all, there would be no tax on the first fifteen thousand made. Why and how is that fair, and how would that work? My answer is every person in the U.S. that makes fifteen thousand or less is at, or below the government poverty level, and is getting all kinds of hand outs already. Besides that, they will spend nearly 100% of that money just to survive, and in fact would still be paying some taxes with the 5% federal sales tax. Anyone making more than that would still fall in that same category of spending.

Federal tax chart	
$0 - $15,000	0%
$15,000.01-$30,000	5%
$30,000.01 - $60.000	10%
$60,000.01 - $150,000	15%
$150,000.01 - $500,000	20%
$500,000.01 & up	25%

After that if you made $30,000, you would only be taxed 5% on the last $15,000, which would actually be .025%. Rather then going through every tax group, I'll show you a couple more. Let's say you make $75,000; that would put you in the 15% bracket. You would pay 0% on your first $15,000 and 5% on your next $15,000, 10% on the next $30,000 and 15% on your last $15,000. When all is said and done, your total taxes would be $6,000 for a total of .08% in taxes. What would a millionaire pay on a one million dollar salary? They would pay $212,250 dollars in taxes or .2122%

Oh what the hell! What would Alex Rodriguez of the New York Yankees pay in one year? His total would be $6,875,000 or .2486%, but don' feel bad for him; he would still clear $21,125,000 or about $130,401.20 a game with this plan. He makes more in one three hour game than 96% of the U.S. population makes all year. Don't get me wrong; I love baseball and A-Rod, but there is something wrong when a man makes more money playing a game than someone who saves our lives; think about it.

How would it work with people such as sub contractors that get a 1099 at the end of the year? The banks would be set up to cash company checks that are for sub contractors. These companies would have special checks with the 1099 code on the check. You would then have to swipe your federal ID card at the bank, and the information that you set up, will automatically tell the bank your current status, take out the taxes and retirement, and give you what's left. Basically, you will be paid like any employee in a normal business except you won't have taxes taken out until you cash your check. You won't file a 1099 at the end of the year, because every time you get paid, it will be with a 1099 check.

Below is an example of what a W2 might look like with your federal ID and retirement account number on it.

Employer Name			W2
Name	Imus	B	Smiling
	First	Middle	Last
Date of Birth	1/1/1992		
	123 First St.		
City	New York	Zip Code	12345
State	New York		
Social Security #	not needed if born after 01/01/94		
Fed ID#	123-45-6789-010192		
Ret. Acct #	***********-1234		

Below is an example of what a pay stub might look like with your retirement account setup.

Sam's Burger Joint	Jan 07	2009		Ck# 1872
123 Hamburger Lane	Imus	B.	Smiling	
San Francisco, Calif.		Year to date		
12345		$200.00	Wages	$200.00
		$10.00	Federal tax	$0.00
		$10.00	State tax	$10.00
Fed ID #	123-45-6789-010192		Ret. Acct.	$15.30
Ret. Acct #	***********-1234		Additional to Ret.	$10.00
Total to Ret. Acct.	$40.60	$40.60	Check Amount	$164.70

It's your money; shouldn't you be able to keep it, and build it up as much as you like? Wouldn't you like to know exactly how much you are going to retire with? And finally, wouldn't you like to be able to leave what's left to your loved ones?

Jobs

I can and will create millions of American jobs instantly by offering a free trip home for all illegal aliens. There are more than 10 million illegal aliens working in this country, doing jobs that we were doing, and its time to get our jobs back. I know this will upset a lot of people, mostly in the south western United States and Florida who are legal immigrants, but that's too bad; the law is the law. If we give amnesty every time we find millions or even thousands of illegal people, what's to stop them from coming? They have to go back. That's all there is to it. I don't mean to be so harsh, but the law is the law.

I also have a plan to put millions of people to work by building a new high speed rail system coast to coast, north to south, and crisscrossing America. We have to have a new way to travel with the price of oil so high and in short supply. The high cost of air travel and the fact that we are going to have a tougher time finding an alternative fuel for airplanes, supports this demand. If we can't develop a less expensive alternative fuel, we will have to find a new way to travel. I will talk more on this later in transportation.

I have seen an idea for an electric magnetic motor made in Australia, as stated earlier, on the internet. That technology could change the world, and create millions of jobs all across America, as well as cut our dependency on foreign oil and fossil fuels. For every job you cut by technology, you create another. Someone has to build and service these mini power plants.

I would raise minimum wage to $8.25 an hour, which I believe is still to low; however, with my idea for the future and future growth of America, it would make $8.25 an hour seem more like $10.00 an hour. Raising minimum wage would help offset the taxes lost by cutting taxes.

Conversions for autos to run on hydrogen instead of or mixed with gas, would temporarily put hundreds of thousands to work. Auto makers will soon be hiring thousands to go back to work with the new technology. There is plenty to do, and no time to waste.

Enuff is Enuff
Vote for Huff

Housing

I would implement a mortgage rate plan fixed at 5% for any legal resident with a valid Federal ID card. Any rate higher than 5.304% on a 30 year mortgage, you are paying more in interest than you are for your home. This makes no sense to me, but that's the price of business in America.

At a 5% interest rate, more Americans would be able to afford housing. This would make housing reasonable to many Americans, and create more construction jobs. However, that rate should be limited to one loan, per Federal ID number; in other words, no slum lording off this rate.

Ok, so you don't want the government running everything, including your mortgage banking. Well I've got news for you, they already do. Who loans money to the banks at a lower rate? The Feds. Who bails out banks when they screw up? The Feds. Who insures the banks? The Feds. Who pays for all the mistakes? We do.

Don't tell me you don't want government running the banks because they already do. They just don't do a good job of it.

Five percent is a good fair rate and a good thing for everyone. If you have a $100,000 mortgage at 6% thirty year fixed, you would be paying $599.55 a month. Now take that same loan at 5%, and you would be paying $536.82 a month; a savings of $62.73 a month, and over $22,000 in interest.

As I said earlier about the 5% tax rate, the same rule would apply here. If the value goes up, so does the profit. The interest rate should remain the same. Economists love playing with the rates, and would put me to shame with all their rhetoric, but I think they're wrong. Why do they feel they have to change the rates up and down? Leave the rates alone.

At this proposed fixed rate, banks could only compete to give you better closing costs. Who wins here? We do.

Enuff is Enuff
Vote for Huff

Immigration

Our fathers and grandfathers didn't die for nothing. This is America, and the language is English, period. If you don't like it, go back to where you came from. I can't stand going to a fast food restaurant and ordering something different from the regular menu when there is a non-English speaking kitchen staff. Almost every time, they get it wrong. The food waste must be so high, it's disgusting. If you want to be a legal citizen of the United States of America, then you better learn English. No English, no federal ID card. This is not the United States of Mexico. I don't care who this pisses off. This is the only way it should be. This is our land. We've defended it for years, and if I were President, you bet your ass I would support this bill.

Also, we need to slow down immigration before it's too late. This country is becoming over populated way to fast, and we need to slow it down. With jobs already hard to find, and the economy at a stand still, we need to take care of our own people first.

We also need to change the law on births in America. Just because you are born here should not be an automatic entitlement to American citizenship, unless at least one parent is a legal citizen. There is no reason to grant citizenship to an illegal immigrant child, just because their parent crossed the border to give birth. It's a bad law, and needs to be changed.

Currently, there are just over 3.5 million square miles of land in the U.S. with a population of just short of 304 million people; that's about 87 people per square mile. If it weren't for cities like New York, Chicago, L.A. and a few others, we would be crowded together with nowhere to go. Think about that for a minute. That is one person per seven and a third acres, or the equivalent of a square measuring 566' by 566' or close to the size of your average Wal-Mart including the parking lot. We need to slow down immigration now.

According to the census bureau, the population doubled from 1900 to 1950; that's fifty years with two world wars. Then, it doubled again from 1950 to 2006; at that rate, about the year 2050 we will have approximately 600,000,000 people in the United States alone, with no place to farm and nowhere to grow food.

We will have fewer trees to produce oxygen because we will be clearing more, and more land as we keep building. By the time we figure out that we are running out of land to harvest, it will be too late. We need to slow down the birth rates as well as immigration. This will be a very serious problem in the not too distant future.

In the very near future, we will all be living like we're in a major city, building up because there is no more room to grow out. With road rage the way it is now, just wait fifty years. I feel so sorry for our kids.

I don't hate Mexicans; they're not the only illegal aliens here in the states. They just happen to be the largest population. They have cost us the most money, due to education, health care, and crime. Not to mention the fact that you can't put a label on anything without it being written in both English and Spanish. That is just plain wrong. If we give amnesty to illegal aliens, then we might as well give amnesty to all criminals too. The law is the law and it applies to all.

Enuff is Enuff
Vote for Huff

Health Care

I believe there should be universal health care for all Americans. There is no reason for not having it. When you're sick, your sick, and you need help. You should be able to get it.

One way we could lower the cost of health care is by letting more people into the Medical schools. The decision about these numbers is left up to the Medical Accreditation Board. They control the number of medical schools and the number of students accepted to these institutions of learning. Each year the board sets a limit on the number of students that they will allow into these accredited universities. The board also controls how many Colleges of Medicine are accredited and permitted to educate.

This restriction reduces the number of doctors, nurses, and other medical professionals that work in this industry. With so few certified medical professionals, this reduces the amount of competition in the medical industry, creating a monopoly. The concept of a monopoly goes against the American way of allowing competition and free enterprise. So why is this monopoly allowed to continue?

I would also put a cap on malpractice suits, which would help to keep cost down. Medical insurance is ridiculously high due to blood thirsty lawyers that sue for their financial gain not yours. Doctors would much rather see you healthy, than in pain, disabled or dead.

Too much money is being wasted by insurance companies that find every reason in the world to charge you, but not cover you. We need to eliminate the middle man, and bill the government directly. No more wasting money on different coverage's, and deductibles. We need to come up with a fair way to make it work: such as $25 office visits and $100 per day hospital visits; not too expensive, but enough to help offset the cost, and keep the hypochondriacs from going all the time.

I also plan to take the former IRS agents, and employ them as health care agents. This would ensure the government isn't being over charged by doctors and hospitals and keeping it more affordable.

For funding health care, I would propose a federal lottery. This lottery would be much larger than Mega Millions and Power Ball, because it would be in all 50 states. This lottery would generate enough money to subsidize health care. Any state not willing to participate in the lottery would not get the health care benefits.

I believe the constitution doesn't allow for federal lotteries, but we can always amend the constitution. It just makes sense to me. This is a new America, not the old one which was written before electricity. Come on, give me a break. Times have changed, and we have to change with it. After all, you would be donating for a good cause with possible financial benefits.

I don't think the health care lottery would hurt the education lottery that much; however, I do believe it would lose some. Both education lotteries would still draw plenty of interest, depending on the size of their jackpot.

There also needs to be lottery reform to make sure the money goes where it's supposed to go. What I mean by this is that government is not disbursing the money fairly, and is holding back money. I will explain more on that later in the lottery reform section.

The government should do everything possible to help kids who want to become doctors, and dedicate their lives to saving ours, and making us better. We should help them with their schooling, and make sure to keep college loans at a low reasonable rate. If anyone wants to be a doctor just for the money, shame on them. They should go into politics.

Enuff is Enuff
Vote for Huff

Energy

Are you listening to these guys talk about energy independence? What energy independence? Barack Obama and John McCain both are saying it, and in the same breath, they say that the auto makers need to make more fuel efficient cars. Did you hear that? More **fuel** efficient cars. How is that energy independence? They're already lying to us. Give me a break.

We need to get off the oil, and start using Hydrogen or electric, period. No more ethanol that has helped in the rise of the cost of food, and no more fossil fuels. We need a clean, cheaper way of transportation. Quit lying to us.

It's not the automakers that are at fault. It's the government and the oil companies. The oil companies don't want to add hydrogen fueling stations at every gas station because of the high cost to install them. Why are they getting subsidies?

We need a new way to create energy. We can put a man on the moon, land a space craft on Mars, and build a space station in outer space. Don't tell me we can't make a car to run on water because we can.

There are many new ways that we can power the cars of tomorrow and convert the cars of today. It is a simple process to make hydrogen from water, but the challenge is to make the hydrogen on demand. This can be done. One reason the government doesn't want this process is because they feel that they won't be able to tax it. If you could just put tap water into your car, the government would lose all the tax money from fuel.

No tax on fuel? Why, that would take away from the roads. Well I'm no spring chicken but, we built the entire United States on less tax money than they charge us now, and way before the gas tax was ever implemented. Of course they won't tell us that, but I'll guarantee you that that's the biggest reason for it to not happen.

Now my thinking on this is that they're wrong. People who are traveling will have to fill up on water and it's not just tap water that is used; there is a little more to it than that. There is supposedly a mixture of water and salt or baking soda, and its best used without the chlorine in tap water according to plans that I have read. So you see there is a process to it.

I'm sure that there might have to be a special way to store it, and agitate it to keep the salt or baking soda from settling. It doesn't have to be treated water just filtered, so most people won't want the hassle of making their own, and would probably buy it at a gas station if it were at a reasonable price. The potential is there. So what are we waiting for?

Also, when it comes to the price of gas, more than half of the money spent on gas goes overseas. We need to keep our money here. Most of the money that we would save on fuel, would be spent right here in our own country. This would be a big boost for our economy and the tax base. If Washington could get their heads out of their asses, they could see it.

Another idea I have thought about for years was the electric car, and how we could make it work. My idea for the electric car was to convert and/or install millions of electric parking meters that would serve as chargers for your car. Plug your car into the new electric parking meters deposit your money and charge your car while you are parked. However with the potential of hydrogen, I think that idea has to go on the back burner for now. This would be more costly than trying the hydrogen system, but I thought of this thirty years ago when we had the first shortage.

Another idea I have had for years is a new system of battery powered cars. The electric cars of today use batteries hooked in series to create higher voltage. For those of you that don't know what hooked in series means? Hooked in series is what you do when you put more than one battery in a flashlight. You install the batteries in the same direction which means that you are putting a positive against a negative together leaving a positive and negative on opposite ends. If you put two double AA batteries at 1.5 volts each. You would then have three volts of power in the flashlight.

In cars today many hook six or more twelve volt batteries in series for 72 or more volts of power. These batteries are heavy and hard to get in and out. The idea I came up with would take a whole lot of retooling by both auto makers and battery manufacturers, but it could easily be done. With all the new technology of batteries we now have. With the batteries lasting longer and staying stronger its time to come up with a new standard one size fits all battery. I have the design for this and it could work. Instead of filling up with gas you could stop at a charging station and replace and go in about the same time it takes to fill up with gas. How is that you ask? I could tell you, but then I'd have to kill you. I'm currently trying to write a patent on this idea so you'll have to wait, sorry.

President Bush said that America is addicted to oil. That is not even close to the truth. America is addicted to the automobile not the way it is fueled. The government and the oil companies are the ones who are addicted to oil.

We have many options but no time to waste with a bunch of political bullshit. It's time to start now.

**Enuff is Enuff
Vote for Huff**

Military

It's a shame that any country even needs a military in this day and age, but unfortunately we do. Even if we became the United Countries of the world and we all spoke the same language and had the same currency, as long as one country had a military we all would have a military.

As for us and the situation we're in now, I would pull our troops as soon as possible. I would then give the troops new jobs patrolling our borders. I would not send any new troops over. Once we start taking troops out that would be the end of it. We are not fighting a conventional war. We are in a policing action, and we are losing troops to terrorist not people in uniform.

I would not stand for any terrorist acts against our country, and would strongly advise against it. Any act would result in a lot more **shock and a lot less aw-full** for any country harboring these terrorist.

We need to have better intelligence so we don't put our troops in harms way, or fight a war we shouldn't be fighting. If we know with no uncertainty that we have legitimate reason to go to war, then we go and end it as soon as possible without putting our troops in harms way. In other words I would blow the shit out of them period.

If you're asking me what kind of leader I would be when it comes to war. I can only say that one of my favorite presidents is Harry Truman or dirty Harry as like to think of him, take no shit and end it as soon as possible. I'm not saying I would blow up the world or anything like that but I would make damn sure that if we had no choice but to go to war. I would make sure that it would be pretty much over before I would send any ground troops in.

**Enuff is Enuff
Vote for Huff**

Abortion

As I said earlier in the book, just give me a chance and I'll probably piss you off somewhere in this book. Well this is where I risk putting off half of the United States or most Republicans anyway. This is a horrible topic. Let's face it, nobody likes abortion. Let's hope in this day of modern medicine, people do not view abortion as a means of birth control.

Most abortions are from kids who are either not educated enough about protection or don't practice abstinence. Many parents are still uncomfortable about the topic, so they don't want to take the time to discuss it. Others don't have the time, due to work or other family responsibilities, to sit down and tell their kids how important it is to wait till they have their education. Also a lot of parents think their kids are still too young to hear about it. But the fact is they probably already have.

I also feel very strongly that kids should not be having kids. Since the government has taken on the responsibility of taking care of single or low income parents by subsidizing them with food stamps and other handouts, this is when it becomes a business decision. What I mean by that is that the government will go broke if it continues paying kids to stay home and have kids. Kids having kids is a no win situation.

Most of the time the mothers ends up quitting school and the fathers don't take any responsibility. Then the government ends up paying for the child until he or she is eighteen. When you consider the far reaching fact that children who grow up in broken homes become a higher risk to be in jail, which tax payers also end up paying for. It becomes a vicious cycle that never ends. With that being said, I feel abortion should be legal. The government is not in the business of paying people to have kids.

Children are making a huge mistake thinking that they won't be the one to get pregnant. I'm a guy and I remember being young and pursuing the opposite sex. Guys will say anything to get girls where they want them. Therefore I understand the pressure young women go through.

Although it may go against some religions I also feel that kids should be put on birth control as soon as they start menstruating (but that is just my opinion and should not be a law). Kids should not be having kid's period. It's the parents' job to educate their children. They need to stay in school and get an education to better theirs and our future.

Rather than paying for handouts for these unprepared new parents, I would much rather see our tax dollars go towards education. The parents need to do a better job of parenting, and teach their kids the value of an education. By waiting to have children until you are older and more mature, it will give you the patience you need to raise a child.

If we can do a better job of educating our kids on this subject, abortion will decrease dramatically. It is very hard to be a good parent when you're working all the time just to pay your bills. Something needs to be done. As I stated earlier in immigration. We are over populating way to fast.

Maybe if we had two separate minimum wages, one for those who graduate high school and one much lower for those who don't, we could solve a lot of our problems with teen pregnancy. Keep the rate where it is for those who don't graduate until age 21, and raise it to $8.25 for those who do. That would encourage kids to stay in school. When they realize that by graduating they can make an extra $80 a week or more. They probably would stay and finish school.

Do you want fries with that?

Enuff is Enuff
Vote for Huff

Retirement

Retirement is getting harder and harder to get with companies filing bankruptcy and closing down; people are getting screwed out of their retirement. If it is their only form of retirement then there needs to be something done.

With my plan major companies would save thousands in Social Security and Medicare matching funds. You ask why I would want to save major companies so much money, when we need to raise the cap because the Social Security fund is going broke.

The Social Security fund is going broke because of misuse of funds from our great government. By cutting the cap $1,155.56 each year for the next 50 years, along with changing the Social Security and Medicare system as we now know it. With my plan businesses would come back to the states because it would be more affordable to do business. Why not take the $52,000 off right away? Good question and I'll try to explain.

With my plan, Social Security and matching funds will remain the same up to $50,000 and that money will go directly into the employer's retirement account, including the Medicare portion. How will that work you ask? With the new health care system in place, we won't need Medicare in the same way we do now. However, we will still need it for the disabled and less fortunate. As of now, the current cap is $102,000 so how are we going to take care of the disabled and less fortunate? After the $50,000 cap, employees will pay 1% of their gross income with no cap. That money will go into a fund for the less fortunate such as: handicapped and children left behind due to the sudden departure of a parent or parents.

The reasoning behind the $1,155.56 a year for the next 50 years is there are so many people in the current system; it would take that long to clear it out. However, there are ways to work it out so that we could cut it in half, but that will have to be worked out at a later time after budget research and complicated calculations. If the people already in the system want to opt out for the new system and possibly draw some from both, I'm sure that something could be worked out.

With my plan, you and your employer could invest as much as you want into your retirement fund while you are working, therefore putting money into your account weekly or bi-weekly however you are paid. Once the money is in your account, it stays there until you reach the age of 65 or as early as 55, providing you can survive on a pro rated income, at or above the poverty level until age 100. If your company should go under, you won't lose your retirement money. Just your job.

What I mean by pro rated is with cost of living adjustments figured in. Let's say you want to retire at age 60, and the poverty level is $18,000. This would mean that with the cost of living increases over the next 40 years figured in, you would need less than $500,000 in your retirement account at 4% interest to survive until age 100. After age 100, the government would then take care of you at or above the poverty level. I will show you how easy it is to save $500,000 over a life time of work even at just over $8 an hour in the next chapter on Social Security.

Retirement is one reason that the cost of consumer products is so high. When major companies offer big retirement plans to lure in qualified personnel, the cost of the product inevitably goes up. As the company grows older, more and more people retire from that company. The cost of paying for these retired employees then goes into the cost of the product.

With my plan, if a company offers a retirement incentive, they could do it by contributing to your personal retirement fund. Once in there, it would stay in your account no matter what. This would save companies a lot of money, making it easy to do business here in the states, and help to create more jobs. It is a win, win situation.

Once you retire, your company will no longer have to pay you or your beneficiary because you have already been paid. Companies can cut ties with you and start over with your replacement. No longer will they have to worry about paying double or triple. My plan would save companies and consumers a lot of money.

Please read the next chapter on Social Security for more information on your retirement.

Social Security

Totally change the system from top to bottom. My system would actually lower the cap that is in place now. Part of the reason big companies are leaving the United States is the cost of doing business. With matching funds, and all of the insurance problems such as workman's compensation, it's no wonder they leave. With this plan, I'll show you how we can lower the amount all the way around and still come out ahead. My plan would allow you to retire at age 55 if you so desired, providing you could live with the balance in your account. With your Social Security Medicare tax withheld exactly as it is today, the 7.65% from you and your employer would go into an account of your choosing that could not be touched until you reach age 55. If by age 55, you have enough saved to average you at or above poverty level with cost of living increases included, for the next 45 years, then you would be free to retire.

Should you die before age 100, the remainder of the fund would go to your heirs. If you should live passed the age of 100, happy birthday the government will take care of you at or above the poverty level until your death. Age 100 is based on 20 years above average life expectancy, and could go up or down with average life expectancy. However, the new system would not help people late in age now, so unfortunately, for the next 50 years there will have to be some sort of way to compensate those already in the system as said in the last chapter.

With my system, the 1% employee tax after the $50,000 cap would help the less fortunate and guarantee that those in the system already live at 10% above the poverty level until their death. With the amount of money already in the system each year for the next fifty years should get easier each year.

Here are some tables showing you how much you should have at different levels of income. These tables are simple interest at 4% and 6% annually just to give you an idea of what you could have.

Notice the yearly salary, and then notice the interest on the savings after 50 years. At $8.17 per hour for a 40 hour week your gross pay would be $326.80 for the week. Take the gross pay times 7.65% and you have $25 plus the matching funds of the employer and you then have $50 per week which works out to be $2600 per year.

	Age 18 $50.00 per week		Age 18 $50.00 per week
$2,600.00		$2,600.00	
$0.04	$8.17 per hour	$0.06	$8.17 per hour
$2,704.00		$2,756.00	
$2,600.00	Age 19	$2,600.00	Age 19
$5,304.00	weekly salary $326.80	$5,356.00	weekly salary $326.80
$0.04	years salary $16,993.60	$0.06	years salary $16,993.60
$5,516.16		$5,677.36	
$2,600.00	Age 20	$2,600.00	Age 20
$8,116.16		$8,277.36	
$0.04		$0.06	

$8,440.81		$8,774.00	
$2,600.00	Age 21	$2,600.00	Age 21
$11,040.81		$11,374.00	
$0.04		$0.06	
$11,482.44		$12,056.44	
$2,600.00	Age 22	$2,600.00	Age 22
$14,082.44		$14,656.44	
$0.04		$0.06	
$14,645.74		$15,535.83	
$2,600.00	Age 23	$2,600.00	Age 23
$17,245.74		$18,135.83	
$0.04		$0.06	
$17,935.57		$19,223.98	
$2,600.00	Age 24	$2,600.00	Age 24
$20,535.57		$21,823.98	
$0.04		$0.06	
$21,356.99		$23,133.42	
$2,600.00	Age 25	$2,600.00	Age 25
$23,956.99		$25,733.42	
$0.04		$0.06	
$24,915.27		$27,277.42	
$2,600.00	Age 26	$2,600.00	Age 26
$27,515.27		$29,877.42	
$0.04		$0.06	
$28,615.88		$31,670.07	
$2,600.00	Age 27	$2,600.00	Age 27
$31,215.88		$34,270.07	
$0.04		$0.06	
$32,464.51		$36,326.27	
$2,600.00	Age 28	$2,600.00	Age 28
$35,064.51		$38,926.27	
$0.04		$0.06	

$36,467.09		$41,261.85	
$2,600.00	Age 29	$2,600.00	Age 29
$39,067.09		$43,861.85	
$0.04		$0.06	
$40,629.78		$46,493.56	
$2,600.00	Age 30	$2,600.00	Age 30
$43,229.78		$49,093.56	
$0.04		$0.06	
$44,958.97		$52,039.17	
$2,600.00	Age 31	$2,600.00	Age 31
$47,558.97		$54,639.17	
$0.04		$0.06	
$49,461.33		$57,917.52	
$2,600.00	Age 32	$2,600.00	Age 32
$52,061.33		$60,517.52	
$0.04		$0.06	
$54,143.78		$64,148.57	
$2,600.00	Age 33	$2,600.00	Age 33
$56,743.78		$66,748.57	
$0.04		$0.06	
$59,013.53		$70,753.49	
$2,600.00	Age 34	$2,600.00	Age 34
$61,613.53		$73,353.49	
$0.04		$0.06	
$64,078.07		$77,754.70	
$2,600.00	Age 35	$2,600.00	Age 35
$66,678.07		$80,354.70	
$0.04		$0.06	
$69,345.20		$85,175.98	
$2,600.00	Age 36	$2,600.00	Age 36
$71,945.20		$87,775.98	
$0.04		$0.06	

$74,823.00		$93,042.54	
$2,600.00	Age 37	$2,600.00	Age 37
$77,423.00		$95,642.54	
$0.04		$0.06	
$80,519.92		$101,381.09	
$2,600.00	Age 38	$2,600.00	Age 38
$83,119.92		$103,981.09	
$0.04		$0.06	
$86,444.72		$110,219.95	
$2,600.00	Age 39	$2,600.00	Age 39
$89,044.72		$112,819.95	
$0.04		$0.06	
$92,606.51		$119,589.15	
$2,600.00	Age 40	$2,600.00	Age 40
$95,206.51		$122,189.15	
$0.04		$0.06	
$99,014.77		$129,520.50	
$2,600.00	Age 41	$2,600.00	Age 41
$101,614.77			$132,120.50
$0.04		$0.06	
$105,679.36		$140,047.73	
$2,600.00	Age 42	$2,600.00	Age 42
$108,279.36		$142,647.73	
$0.04		$0.06	
$112,610.54		$151,206.60	
$2,600.00	Age 43	$2,600.00	Age 43
$115,210.54		$153,806.60	
$0.04		$0.06	
$119,818.96		$163,034.99	
$2,600.00	Age 44	$2,600.00	Age 44
$122,418.96		$165,634.99	
$0.04		$0.06	

$127,315.72		$175,573.09	
$2,600.00	Age 45	$2,600.00	Age 45
$129,915.72		$178,173.09	
$0.04		$0.06	
$135,112.34		$188,863.48	
$2,600.00	Age 46	$2,600.00	Age 46
$137,712.34		$191,463.48	
$0.04		$0.06	
$143,220.84		$202,951.28	
$2,600.00	Age 47	$2,600.00	Age 47
$145,820.84		$205,551.28	
$0.04		$0.06	
$151,653.67		$217,884.36	
$2,600.00	Age 48	$2,600.00	Age 48
$154,253.67		$220,484.36	
$0.04		$0.06	
$160,423.82		$233,713.42	
$2,600.00	Age 49	$2,600.00	Age 49
$163,023.82		$236,313.42	
$0.04		$0.06	
$169,544.77		$250,492.23	
$2,600.00	Age 50	$2,600.00	Age 50
$172,144.77		$253,092.23	
$0.04		$0.06	
$179,030.56		$268,277.76	
$2,600.00	Age 51	$2,600.00	Age 51
$181,630.56		$270,877.76	
$0.04		$0.06	
$188,895.78		$287,130.43	
$2,600.00	Age 52	$2,600.00	Age 52
$191,495.78		$289,730.43	
$0.04		$0.06	

$199,155.62		$307,114.25	
$2,600.00	Age 53	$2,600.00	Age 53
$201,755.62		$309,714.25	
$0.04		$0.06	
$209,825.84		$328,297.11	
$2,600.00	Age 54	$2,600.00	Age 54
$212,425.84		$330,897.11	
$0.04		$0.06	
$220,922.87		$350,750.94	
$2,600.00	Age 55	$2,600.00	Age 55
$223,522.87		$353,350.94	
$0.04		$0.06	
$232,463.79		$374,551.99	
$2,600.00	Age 56	$2,600.00	Age 56
$235,063.79		$377,151.99	
$0.04		$0.06	
$244,466.34		$399,781.11	
$2,600.00	Age 57	$2,600.00	Age 57
$247,066.34		$402,381.11	
$0.04		$0.06	
$256,948.99		$426,523.98	
$2,600.00	Age 58	$2,600.00	Age 58
$259,548.99		$429,123.98	
$0.04		$0.06	
$269,930.95		$454,871.42	
$2,600.00	Age 58	$2,600.00	Age 58
$272,530.95		$457,471.42	
$0.04		$0.06	
$283,432.19		$484,919.70	
$2,600.00	Age 59	$2,600.00	Age 59
$286,032.19		$487,519.70	
$0.04		$0.06	

$297,473.48		$516,770.88	
$2,600.00	Age 60	$2,600.00	Age 60
$300,073.48		$519,370.88	
$0.04		$0.06	
$312,076.42		$550,533.14	
$2,600.00	Age 61	$2,600.00	Age 61
$314,676.42		$553,133.14	
$0.04		$0.06	
$327,263.48		$586,321.12	
$2,600.00	Age 62	$2,600.00	Age 62
$329,863.48		$588,921.12	
$0.04		$0.06	
$343,058.02		$624,256.39	
$2,600.00	Age 63	$2,600.00	Age 63
$345,658.02		$626,856.39	
$0.04		$0.06	
$359,484.34		$664,467.77	
$2,600.00	Age 64	$2,600.00	Age 64
$362,084.34		$667,067.77	
$0.04		$0.06	
$376,567.71		$707,091.84	
$2,600.00	Age 65	$2,600.00	Age 65
$379,167.71		$709,691.84	
$0.04		$0.06	
$394,334.42		$752,273.35	
$2,600.00	Age 66	$2,600.00	Age 66
$396,934.42		$754,873.35	
$0.04		$0.06	
$412,811.79		$800,165.75	
$2,600.00	Age 67		Age 67
$415,411.79		$802,765.75	
$0.04		$0.06	

$432,028.27	total	$850,931.70	Total
$0.04		$0.06	
$17,281.13	Interest per year at the end	$51,055.90	Interest per year at the end

Isn't it funny how the interest at 4% is more than your yearly salary after 50 years of hard work? At six percent, it is nearly double that, and this doesn't include the money that is in your account. Wow! We're getting screwed!

This is why with my plan, instead of companies and employees paying Social Security and Medicare up to $102,000, we could lower the cap giving breaks to both companies and employees; putting more money in your pocket, and helping to bring business back to the United States. Instead of big companies moving to other countries to avoid this huge bill, they would then stay here, and all the others would move back.

The next chart shows how much you would have with as little as $18.92 an hour which is slightly under $40,000 per year for fifty years. What this means to me is we could cut the cap in half, and you could still retire a millionaire. Think about this; if people retired with a fixed income higher than what they made working, not only would it open a job where he/she retired from but they would probably travel and spend their money, and help support the tourism business. It's a win, win situation.

Where is our money? What the hell have they done with it? This is absurd; no wonder the American people and businesses are **FED-UP.**

$6,018.13	Age 18 $115.74 per week	$6,018.13	Age 18 $115.74 per week
$0.04	$18.92 per hour	$0.06	$18.92 per hour
$6,258.86		$6,379.22	
$6,018.13	Age 19	$6,018.13	Age 19
$12,276.99	weekly salary $756.80	$12,397.35	weekly salary $756.80
$0.04	years salary $39,353.60	$0.06	years salary $39,353.60
$12,768.06		$13,141.19	
$6,018.13	Age 20	$6,018.13	Age 20
$18,786.19		$19,159.32	
$0.04		$0.06	
$19,537.64		$20,308.88	
$6,018.13	Age 21	$6,018.13	Age 21
$25,555.77		$26,327.01	
$0.04		$0.06	
$26,578.00		$27,906.63	
$6,018.13	Age 22	$6,018.13	Age 22
$32,596.13		$33,924.76	
$0.04		$0.06	
$33,899.98		$35,960.24	
$6,018.13	Age 23	$6,018.13	Age 23
$39,918.11		$41,978.37	
$0.04		$0.06	
$41,514.83		$19,223.98	
$6,018.13	Age 24	$6,018.13	Age 24
$47,532.96		$50,515.21	
$0.04		$0.06	
$49,434.28		$53,546.12	

$6,018.13	Age 25	$6,018.13	Age 25
$55,452.41		$59,564.25	
$0.04		$0.06	
$57,670.51		$63,138.10	
$6,018.13	Age 26	$2,600.00	Age 26
$63,688.64		$69,156.23	
$0.04		$0.06	
$66,236.18		$73,305.61	
$6,018.13	Age 27	$2,600.00	Age 27
$72,254.31		$79,323.74	
$0.04		$0.06	
$75,144.49		$84,083.16	
$6,018.13	Age 28	$6,018.13	Age 28
$81,162.62		$90,101.29	
$0.04		$0.06	
$84,409.12		$95,507.37	
$6,018.13	Age 29	$6,018.13	Age 29
$90,427.25		$101,525.50	
$0.04		$0.06	
$94,044.34		$107,617.03	
$6,018.13	Age 30	$6,018.13	Age 30
$100,062.47		$113,635.16	
$0.04		$0.06	
$104,064.97		$120,453.27	
$6,018.12	Age 31	$6,018.12	Age 31
$110,083.09		$126,471.39	
$0.04		$0.06	
$114,486.41		$134,059.67	
$6,018.12	Age 32	$6,018.12	Age 32
$120,504.53		$140,077.79	
$0.04		$0.06	
$125,324.71		$148,482.46	

$6,018.12	Age 33	$6,018.12	Age 33
$131,342.83		$154,500.58	
$0.04		$0.06	
$136,596.55		$163,770.61	
$6,018.12	Age 34	$6,018.12	Age 34
$142,614.67		$169,788.73	
$0.04		$0.06	
$148,319.25		$179,976.06	
$6,018.12	Age 35	$6,018.12	Age 35
$154,337.37		$185,994.18	
$0.04		$0.06	
$160,510.87		$197,153.83	
$6,018.12	Age 36	$6,018.12	Age 36
$166,528.99		$203,171.95	
$0.04		$0.06	
$173,190.15		$215,362.27	
$6,018.12	Age 37	$6,018.12	Age 37
$179,208.27		$221,380.39	
$0.04		$0.06	
$186,376.60		$234,663.21	
$6,018.12	Age 38	$6,018.12	Age 38
$192,394.72		$240,681.33	
$0.04		$0.06	
$200,090.51		$255,122.21	
$6,018.12	Age 39	$6,018.12	Age 39
$206,108.63		$261,140.33	
$0.04		$0.06	
$214,352.97		$276,808.75	
$6,018.12	Age 40	$6,018.12	Age 40
$220,371.09		$282,826.87	
$0.04		$0.06	
$229,185.94		$299,796.48	

$6,018.12	Age 41	$6,018.12	Age 41
$235,204.06		$305,814.60	
$0.04		$0.06	
$244,612.22		$324,163.48	
$6,018.12	Age 42	$6,018.12	Age 42
$250,630.34		$330,181.60	
$0.04		$0.06	
$260,655.55		$349,992.49	
$6,018.12	Age 43	$6,018.12	Age 43
$266,673.67		$356,010.61	
$0.04		$0.06	
$277,340.62		$377,371.25	
$6,018.12	Age 44	$6,018.12	Age 44
$283,358.74		$383,389.37	
$0.04		$0.06	
$294,693.09		$406,392.73	
$6,018.12	Age 45	$6,018.12	Age 45
$300,711.21		$412,410.85	
$0.04		$0.06	
$312,739.66		$437,155.50	
$6,018.12	Age 46	$6,018.12	Age 46
$318,757.78		$443,173.62	
$0.04		$0.06	
$331,508.09		$469,764.04	
$6,018.12	Age 47	$6,018.12	Age 47
$337,526.21		$475,782.16	
$0.04		$0.06	
$351,027.26		$504,329.09	
$6,018.12	Age 48	$6,018.12	Age 48
$357,045.38		$510,347.21	
$0.04		$0.06	
$371,327.19		$540,968.04	

$6,018.12	Age 49	$6,018.12	Age 49
$377,345.31		$546,986.16	
$0.04		$0.06	
$392,439.13		$579,805.33	
$6,018.12	Age 50	$6,018.12	Age 50
$398,457.26			
$0.04		$0.06	
$414,395.55		$620,972.87	
$6,018.12	Age 51	$6,018.12	Age 51
$420,413.67		$626,990.99	
$0.04		$0.06	
$437,230.21		$664,610.45	
$6,018.12	Age 52	$6,018.12	Age 52
$443,248.33		$670,628.57	
$0.04		$0.06	
$460,978.27		$710,866.28	
$6,018.12	Age 53	$6,018.12	Age 53
$466,996.39		$716,884.40	
$0.04		$0.06	
$485,676.24		$759,897.47	
$6,018.12	Age 54	$6,018.12	Age 54
$491,694.36		$765,915.59	
$0.04		$0.06	
$511,362.14		$811,870.52	
$6,018.12	Age 55	$6,018.12	Age 55
$517,380.26		$817,888.64	
$0.04		$0.06	
$538,075.47		$866,961.96	
$6,018.12	Age 56	$6,018.12	Age 56
$544,093.59		$872,980.08	
$0.04		$0.06	
$565,857.33		$925,358.89	

$6,018.12	Age 57	$6,018.12	Age 57
$571,875.45		$931,377.01	
$0.04		$0.06	
$594,750.47		$987,259.63	
$6,018.12	Age 58	$6,018.12	Age 58
$600,768.59		$993,277.75	
$0.04		$0.06	
$624,799.33		$1,052,874.41	
$6,018.12	Age 58	$6,018.12	Age 58
$630,817.45		$1,058,892.53	
$0.04		$0.06	
$656,050.15		$1,122,426.08	
$6,018.12	Age 59	$6,018.12	Age 59
$662,068.27		$1,128,444.20	
$0.04		$0.06	
$688,551.00		$1,196,150.86	
$6,018.12	Age 60	$6,018.12	Age 60
$694,569.12		$1,202,168.98	
$0.04		$0.06	
$722,351.88		$1,274,299.11	
$6,018.12	Age 61	$6,018.12	Age 61
$728,370.00		$1,280,317.23	
$0.04		$0.06	
$757,504.80		$1,357,136.27	
$6,018.12	Age 62	$6,018.12	Age 62
$763,522.92		$1,363,154.39	
$0.04		$0.06	
$794,063.84		$1,444,943.65	
$6,018.12	Age 63	$6,018.12	Age 63
$800,081.96		$1,450,961.77	
$0.04		$0.06	
$832,085.24		$1,538,019.48	

$6,018.12	Age 64	$6,018.12	Age 64
$838,103.36		$1,544,037.60	
$0.04		$0.06	
$871,627.49		$1,636,679.85	
$6,018.12	Age 65	$6,018.12	Age 65
$877,645.61		$1,642,697.97	
$0.04		$0.06	
$912,751.44		$1,741,259.85	
$6,018.12	Age 66	$6,018.12	Age 66
$918,769.56		$1,747,277.97	
$0.04		$0.06	
$955,520.34		$1,852,114.65	
$6,018.12	Age 67		Age 67
$961,538.46		$1,858,132.77	
$0.04		$0.06	
$1,000,000.00	total	$1,969,620.74	total
$0.04		$0.06	
$40,000.00	Interest per year at the end	$118,177.24	Interest per year at the end

Again, after fifty years, the interest is more than your salary; something has to be done. How many people do you know that are millionaires making only $40,000 a year? Not many.

This money would be taxed as a yearly income without taking the retirement tax out. This would give you even more money to live on during your golden years. I want you to spend your retirement money and enjoy your life. By making the most of your retirement, you would be doing your country and you a great service. We can't go on like this forever. We are not stupid people; at some point we have to say enough.

With these charts you can see where you should be based on your age, and wages you have earned. It won't make you happy and you're probably not going to get it back, but it's nice to know how well our government is working for us the tax paying citizens of the United States.

Enuff is Enuff
Vote for Huff

Insurance Reform

Insurance companies would really hate me, but they will survive none the less. They have been living off the government backing them long enough. If it weren't for government, insurance companies would not be where they're at right now. It is because of the government that people are forced to have insurance anyway, even though you are not forced to have health insurance.

Under my plan, insurance companies would no longer be in the health care business because everyone would be covered by the government plan. I'm sure they will try to come up with a way to sell you on some sort of emergency insurance to cover you and your deductible while you're sick or injured and out of work. However, they won't be able to stop you from getting the care you need when you need it most. No more getting dropped after surgeries or long costly diseases, leaving your loved ones to pay the bill.

Insurance is really putting people in a bind. Insurance is becoming a tax that you have to have. From health insurance to auto insurance we are getting screwed. If you have a mortgage, car, or a business, you have to have insurance. Insurance is driving the cost of everything sky high and something needs to be done.

If you are a private company, you are required to have workman's compensation, which doesn't cover you, the owner; this is wrong. If you own multiple vehicles, and are required by the state to have insurance just to have a license, why can't we come up with one insurance policy that covers you and anything that you drive? Insure the licensee to cover the most expensive vehicle, and it would then cover any vehicle you own and list with the insurance company. I have three vehicles: a motorcycle, truck, and a family vehicle; however, I can only drive one at a time, but still pay for all three, and it's killing me that I have to do this.

Another thing, have you tried to get insurance for a young driver these days? Forget it! Over $200 a month just for liability insurance, it's crazy. How can young kids in school afford it? They can't, leaving their parents to help out when they're already strapped for cash; something has to be done.

I understand that they are a risk, but I think that many people that already have licenses can't drive and don't understand the laws of the road. I think that the road test to get your license is way too easy and is not about driving. Who gives a shit if you can parallel park or do a three point turn? I want to know if you can drive a car. The road test should be more like getting a pilots license. You should have to log a certain amount of hours with a certified trainer.

Stay the hell out of the passing lane if you're not passing. That would be the left lane for those of you who don't know. Adjust your side mirrors so you can see what's on the side of you, not so you can see your car. Your car is there; you don't need to see it. Don't change three lanes when you're on vacation, and see a place you want to go to. I see it all the time. Would it kill you to pass it and come back? No, but it might if you don't.

Enuff is Enuff
Vote for Huff

Lottery Reform

The lottery was supposed to be a great way to raise money for the school system, but has become, and has always been, a plan to rip off the people playing and screw the school system. How are they screwing the school system and players you ask?

First of all, when you see the prize for the lottery, let's just say $15,000,000, there is actually $30,000,000. Why is that? When you buy a ticket, 50% goes to the prize pot and the rest goes to the school systems 35%, lottery commission 8%, and the retailer 7% who sells the ticket. This is fine, just what they said it was for. However what they didn't tell you is that when you win and get taxed over 50% on your winnings. That tax money goes into a totally different fund. That is misleading and not right. That money belongs to education as well and needs to stay there.

Why does the government think they can get away with this time and time again and not get caught? Just like the amnesty for illegal alien's bill they tried to sneak by, with the war bill; it is absurd. Sneaky politicians, screwing us again. When are we going to stop electing lawyers to political office? They know how to put words together to make you feel good about getting screwed. Lawyers are killing this country with all their rhetoric. Lawyers make a great living off your tax dollars.

Let's reform the lottery and make it right. Education is very important to our survival and we shouldn't cut it short.

Enuff is Enuff
Vote for Huff

Transportation

The most important thing to do right now is get off our dependency for oil. We must find a way to convert the cars on the road today to an alternative fuel such as hydrogen. I think hydrogen would be the easiest and fastest way to convert the millions of cars on the road today. We can't all afford new cars, but we could afford to convert to hydrogen. There are many plans on the internet available now, but I have not yet tried one. It can be done. Let's get it done.

As I said earlier, a monorail system that uses magnetic, electric or hydrogen power instead of gas or diesel makes for a much cleaner environment. This rail system could have all kinds of possibilities; imagine a rail system that could ship you and your car across the country at speeds of 100 to 200 miles an hour. It can be done. This would create hundreds of thousands of jobs all across the country. Every part of this entire project would be built in America by Americans.

**Enuff is Enuff
Vote for Huff**

Education

Education is the key to the future. We need smaller classrooms, and teachers who are qualified and truly care about their responsibilities as a teacher. Isn't it funny how teachers have to have a Masters degree to work for less than half of what they could get somewhere else with the same degree? We expect so much from our teachers but get mad when they expect our kids to do their work. Why is it that our kids are never wrong and it's always the teachers fault?

Teachers face this challenge with their eyes open but may not anticipate the hurdles that will be thrust in front of them as they try to help their students. Communities need to be a part of the solution, not the predatory lawyer watching, ready to pounce when things go wrong.

We need to keep career oriented classes that give kids a chance to see what the future holds for them. Children haven't changed all that much over time. The technology and tools that they use have, but not every child is headed for college; not every student will be the next doctor or lawyer. We need workers in this country who have initiative and a good work ethic, whether they work with their hands, equipment, or their heads. Why would we eliminate programs where many students find success AND a reason to stay in school?

No Child Left Behind needs to be scrapped; it doesn't work, and it punishes schools and the children who are attending those schools and are doing well. This plan separates students into subgroups, but then states that they should all achieve 100% proficiency; a contradiction from the beginning. When this legislation was approved, who planned how schools would get the financing so that we are equally prepared to teach our students? Equal standards for all children should mean strides that explore their individual strengths, and helps lead them to a productive career, as well as awakening them to the idea of citizenship – being able to give back as well as take.

This is the burden that many teachers are willing to take on, but the ideals of making a difference are blocked by brick walls. Parents need to be proactive partners with teachers, not only during the early learning years, but all the way through high school. Children grow and the bigger they get, the more they say they don't need your help and many parents tend to believe them. This is why there is such a problem in high schools today. Parents react with rage when things go wrong, defending their child as any RESPONSIBLE parent would do. However, not all parents are responsible and expect someone else to solve their child's problems. What is a teacher supposed to do when a parent says "I don't know what to do with them? If you have any ideas, please let me know." Did parenting become a transferable job? Look out teachers....you're doomed to failure when you suddenly have parental rights after 13 or 14 years of ....who knows what?

Also, as I said earlier about lottery taxes, states that have lotteries would have to change their policies on taxes on lottery winnings. Don't call it the education lottery when you take the tax money on the winnings, and use it for other purposes. All taxes on lottery winnings should go to education, period. It should be 25%, not the 50% or more now in place. If I were president, I would work with the governors of all states with lotteries to make sure of it. There would be no misleading state or federal tax on this money; it would all go to the state for education only.

College has to become more affordable and safer to attend. I feel that college should not be the free ride for athletes to go to the pros. Although sports have been in universities from the beginning, I feel that they are taking advantage of these athletes and the athletes are taking advantage of the schools. It has become the minor league for many pro sports and that is a shame. I think that pro sports teams should pay the schools back in a scholarship fund for every athlete they draft or sign on. Not only should the organization reimburse the college for the athlete's cost of school, but double that cost for a non athletic scholarship fund in the name of the athlete for deserving academic achievers. That athlete could endorse the fund to any or all degrees of his or her choice, and would help someone who is not athletic but is in need of financial help.

**Enuff is Enuff
Vote for Huff**

Nuclear Power Plants

We need more. We haven't built any since the seventies. Americans are using more and more electricity every day, there also is a lot more people in America today than there was in the 70's. Nuclear power is clean, safe and efficient. If we built a high speed rail system with electric motors, we would need a way to power it. Nuclear power is the way to do it.

However, we wouldn't need as many new power plants if we went to magnetic or hydrogen power, but we would still need some. Magnetic or hydrogen power could cut the need for electric power from conventional power plants in half, but we have a long way to go for that to happen. With the current population growth, the need for more power is still there.

**Enuff is Enuff
Vote for Huff**

Gay Marriage

I personally don't care who you marry as long as you're happy and productive in society. In other words, it's not the government's business. Many people, me included, don't want to see public show of affection between same sex partners.

As for marriage and the government, I don't think the government should give breaks to people because they're married, just as I feel they shouldn't penalize people for not getting married. Giving people tax breaks for being married, or having kids is not fair to people who don't want to marry or have kids; it's discrimination. Stay out of our personal lives.

Marriage is for anyone who wants it; whether you are black, white, green, or yellow, fat, skinny, tall or short, ugly, beautiful, man or woman, woman and woman, man and man; marriage is not discriminative, people are, and apparently so is our government.

Gun Control

I personally hate guns, but I own one and feel it is your right to own a gun; however, assault rifles and any gun that holds more than eight rounds, I feel should be outlawed. I also feel we need tougher laws on unregistered guns, such as mandatory jail time. If you are caught with an unregistered gun, then you most likely aren't supposed to have one, or you're planning on something illegal. If you are legal, you have nothing to fear by registering your weapons, and if your not, you're going to jail. I would propose a mandatory 30 days for first offence, six months for second offence and five years for third. Four foul balls and your out, life in prison. If this law were to pass, it would give more than a sufficient time period for legal citizens to register their guns or file for special privilege license in the case of collectors who are legal to have weapons.

One of the biggest advocates of guns is the sportsman. What kind of sport is hunting a defenseless animal with an assault rifle anyway? **If you want it to be a sport, hunt a grizzly with a 22 rifle. Now that would be a sport. Better run fast. Guns don't kill people, people kill people. I've heard it all, try using your fist or better yet go back to school, get an education, and learn how to fight with words.**

I understand that people have the right to defend themselves, and I understand their constitutional rights; however, if we make it a mandatory jail sentence for illegal guns that are not registered, then we might stop a lot of violent crimes from happening. If the people understand that they will spend mandatory time in jail for an illegal weapon, then they will be more apt to turn their weapons in for offered cash. We have to do something to get illegal weapons out of the hands of criminals. There will be no penalty for weapons turned in as long as it is done within the given time period of the above said law.

When the second amendment was written, guns were only single shot.

Enuff is Enuff
Vote for Huff

Foreign Policy

We need fair trade, not the free trade that's in place now. How is it fair to trade with countries that have much lower incomes than we do? Our trade with Canada is fine; their income is comparable to ours, unlike Mexico and China which have a much lower pay scale. After all, we don't see Canadians coming here to work but they love to travel here and spend their money.

We need to work with Mexico as well as other countries to improve their wages and then we wouldn't have to worry about them jumping the border so much, to come here illegally and work.

However, we still need to watch the border since Americans seem to love drugs more than they love themselves. It's shameful that America is the biggest buyer of illegal drugs. If you want to get high, get high on life; it's much better.

We need to tax imports the same way they tax our exports. We need to get along with and help other countries in need **but not before taking care of our own first.**

Technology

America used to be the land of pride and innovation. Now we have become the land of greed and over taxation. We need to get it back. Other countries are leaving us behind because our government and big business is holding us back. Honda has developed a car that runs on hydrogen, and is currently working on mini hydrogen units that not only refuel your car with hydrogen, but can also produce heat and electricity for your house. I guess we will be buying more and more things from over seas in our future. This has to stop! Give us the freedom to explore new technology here. We can do it.

How do you stop technology? You can't! But the government and/or some rich company will have you killed if you come up with an idea to change the world. We are not stupid people, and we all have heard the stories of the car that runs on water, the carburetor that gets 100 miles to the gallon, and about magnetic power. That's right; it's all on the internet. You can't stop technology; it's here, but at what cost? If we all had cars that ran on magnetic power, we wouldn't need gas stations. If we all had magnetic generators powering our houses, we wouldn't need power plants or electric companies. We would, however, have a very clean environment, but we would lose millions of millions of jobs all over the world. The rich would really own you then. What would we do? What could we do?

I think something can be done and something should be done. One of the first things that would help is higher wages and less hours of work with a mandatory two week paid vacation. Fair work and fair wages, it may sound dumb to the wealthy but I think it would work.

Imagine six hour shifts at work for the same weekly salary. Making more money for less work, it would work. Four shifts a day would allow companies to hire more people, and give workers more time off for their families, which would have a ripple effect down the line. Better family life, less stress, better sleep, better health, and less crime. I think this would stop a lot of things such as road rage and traffic accidents. People would be better rested and have more time to get around and not rush to do everything.

This would also increase production and quality of products with workers being less fatigued and more focused on their work. Imagine what we could have with magnetic powered or hydrogen autos. We could have lower shipping cost that would keep prices down. We could have a whole new look on the road. No longer will motor companies have to worry about aero dynamics and the E.P.A. we could have cars just like we did back in the fifties all over again. New designs every year that would make people want to buy a new car and boost the economy.

With a new look every year just like it used to be. We would create thousands of new jobs across the country. Gas stations would lose some gas business at first, but it would take years to get rid of the need for gas if ever. Mostly because old car buffs would insist on keeping classics the way they were made, but for the most part, gas stations would stay open as convenient stores which are minimum wage jobs anyway. The auto industry would boom again. This would create higher wages across the board.

I feel that oil companies will still drill for oil. But they will be able to drill here and keep the money here. Oil is used to make all kinds of products that we use in everyday life, and they wouldn't suffer a complete loss.

Electric companies will be around for years it would take time to convert every house into its own little power plant, and somebody has to build these mini electric plants anyway. I would work with electric companies to get involved in that process and install and service them. I believe this could change the world by not polluting the air we need to live. This should be looked at seriously.

As Americans we shouldn't look down on anyone, and we should never look up to anyone except our parents.

**Enuff is Enuff
Vote for Huff**

Final Thoughts

It is not just our federal government that needs to be cleaned up. We need a complete overhaul from top to bottom. There are far too many state, federal, and local employees being paid for what ifs, and we can't afford it. What do I mean by that? Police, FBI, CIA, DSS, probation officers, and the list goes on. They are paid to do absolutely nothing, unless something or someone goes wrong. Yes, we need these agencies. However, some of these employees, I think, are way over paid, as well as some that are under paid.

What would happen if we took the technology we have today and really put it to work? We have GPS and satellite communication. What if we really put it to work?

What if we put GPS in every car of the future? And then programmed them to know every speed limit where you were at. Then we could make it so that you couldn't go faster than ten miles an hour over the speed limit in you car via GPS. What would we as Americans think of that? Would we all bitch about the safety and government control.

Yes, I think we would. But think about the possibilities of what could happen. It is incredible to contemplate it. It would save on accidents, insurance, fines, and taxes, not to mention, it will be a lot harder to have your vehicle stolen. Will it ever get passed? I seriously doubt it.

As far as state taxes and laws go, each state is different. In most states, if not all, one problem that I have is with vehicle registration. Why do we have to pay year after year for the same vehicle? It is just plain wrong. Once you register it in your name that should be it, done. It's yours. You're marked with a plate that you paid for when you registered it with the state. Quit charging us year after year.

The only reason they do this is for income to keep state employees working. Everybody can't work for the government, there would be no one left to pay for it. They should act like any other business, and cut spending by laying them off. Sorry to all of you government employees, but something has to be done.

In my state, I have to pay property taxes every year on my vehicles. Tell me that this is not a bunch of shit. Pretty soon, they'll charge me property tax on the contents in my home. Why not? I own that too. Maybe I'll have to register my sneakers and put a tag on the heel. Why not? They get me around town too. Just one more gripe about taxes. Why do we pay sale tax on the same vehicle every time it gets sold?

I do agree with inspections, for safety reasons. However, when we finally get rid of the emissions with the hydrogen or electric autos, I feel they should drop the cost back to where it was or close to it.

There are many important issues to take care of, all starting with you. It is you who can help change the world we live in. Don't think for one minute that you don't count. You have a voice, use it. Vote, vote, vote!! Don't get caught up in the party system. Listen, and use your own discretion; you're smarter than you think.

Oh I almost forgot. Who would I choose to be my running mate? Well on my short list would be: Spud Webb, Earl

Boykins, and the mayor of Munchkin City. But seriously, I would have to say Jessie Ventura the former Governor of Minnesota or Lou Dobbs from CNN to start with. If you really want change you can believe in, then believe in yourself. Vote Independent and change business as usual.

Thank you so much for taking the time to read this book. I hope you enjoyed it as much as I did writing it. If you enjoyed this book and liked what I had to say. Then please spread the word and help someone else to see what we can do to change the country. It's not too late, but we're getting close. My web site www.Huff4President.com should be up and running with polls, and a blog. I'd love to hear your response to the book and my ideas, as well as your help getting me on the ballot in each state.

Now say the words I like to hear.

If I were elected President, I would work with Oil, Auto, Insurance, and Electric companies and straighten out these issues, and get this started right away.

Thank you
Butch Huff

References

Boortz, Neal and Linder, John, <u>The Fair Tax Book</u>, Regan Books, 2005

www.ingramcontent.com/pod-product-compliance
Lightning Source LLC
Chambersburg PA
CBHW031258280526
45784CB00004B/1899